The Philadelphia Trivia Quiz

By Bernard M. Stiefel

Contributing Editor: William E. Dwyer, Sr.

Normandy Square Publications

Copyright 1984 by Bernard M. Stiefel

Published by Normandy Square Publications
1111 Grand Ave., Suite 200
Kansas City, Mo. 64106

Printed by Walsworth Publishing Co.
Marceline, Mo. 64658

Cover design by Margit Kildahl

Photos courtesy of the Philadelphia Eagles (page 14, bottom);
Broadcast Pioneers Library (page 26, top); WPEN (page 26, bottom); Theater Collection, Free Library of Philadelphia (page
36); *Philadelphia Magazine* (page 46); Stephen Pitcairn (page
56, bottom); Office of the City Representative (page 66, top);
WCAU (page 66, bottom right).

Cover photos, from left: Old Broad Street Station (Free Library
of Philadelphia); Chief Halftown (WPVI-TV); Tug McGraw
celebrating the Phillies' 1980 World Series victory (Wide World
Photos). Top: the Tastykake girls. Bottom: Philadelphia soft
pretzels.

ISBN 0-916399-01-X

This book is dedicated to the memory of my mother and father, Bert and Sam, and to my beautiful daughter, Adrienne.

Acknowledgements

I know that I could not have written this book without the help of a number of very interested and caring people. I would like to offer my sincere appreciation and thanks for their support and contributions.

First, I wish to thank my special contributing editor, Jack Downey, a truly great Philadelphian and a good friend. His knowledge and contacts gathered through his many years at WCAU, in city government, and, more recently, as owner and host of his own fine restaurant, Downey's, has been an important element in making this book authentically Philly.

Next, I would like to acknowledge my very close friend Bill Dwyer, whose tireless efforts as contributing editor made the whole thing work. His relentless pursuit of Philadelphia's famous resulted in the best group of contributing celebrities one could have hoped for. His overall assistance was invaluable, and his sheer determination and energy in finding elusive pieces of information was incredible. Thanks also to Bill's lovely wife, Jean, who not only contributed some questions but also provided the dining room table down at Longport that was used to lay out our work and review our findings.

Special thanks go to my business partner, Steve Kerner, for his help and encouragement all along the way. Without his editing, insights, and suggestions, we would not have made it. I also want to thank Cathy Lobel-Kerner, Steve's wife, for her helpful advice and counsel.

Next, I offer appreciation to my two favorite

Philadelphia lawyers, Larry Rosenwald and my cousin Jay Robert Stiefel. They both, in their own way, added a great deal to the success of this effort.

Along with my good friends Bob Freedman, Bob Wilcox, and their entire staff at SZF Advertising in New York, I would like to salute the following individuals who went out of their way to provide a great deal of assistance: Joan Cherry, Gerry Duclow, Elaine Ebo, Bill Epstein, Jim Gallagher, Marcy Guberman, Bill Hart, William Jones, Arthur Moore, Patricia Proscino, Henry Simpson, Tom Stanley, Fred Voigt, and Frank Walker.

Thanks also go to Charlie Balkin, Joe Berkery, Bill Branson, Don Cameron, Cathy Conway, Lynda Dartnell, Jerry Donahue, Joan English, Bonnie Erickson, Diane Glynn, Judith Hall, Wade Harrison, Rene Heckman, Felicia Hickey, Dan Ingersoll, Pat Kelker, Chris Legault, Shelly Margolus, Willie O'Neill, Frank Palumbo Jr., Ray Parillo, Richie Powers, Mary Ann Promos, Ronald Robbins, Charles Santore, Ben Sharav, Phil Sheridan, Darryl Stackhouse, George Watson, John Paul Weber, Jane Yagerhofer, and Joyce Zogott.

Finally, none of this would have happened if Paul Blackman and Richard Zoglin, of Normandy Square Publications, had not done the same for their home town of Kansas City and decided to be our publishers.

Contents

Preface

Bernard ("Sonny") Stiefel is a born and bred Philadelphian. His father was Sam Stiefel, owner of a chain of movie houses scattered throughout the city. His cousin was State Sen. Israel Stiefel, who, from 1936 to 1964, represented his North Philadelphia district in Harrisburg, where he did much to raise the level of historic consciousness in the state. In this family environment, "Sonny" was bound to be interested in the city of Philadelphia and its historical background, and he began unwittingly collecting data for this book even as a child.

I too am a Philadelphian by birth and upbringing. When I was a boy attending Robert Morris Public School at 26th and Thompson St., and then Central High School when it was downtown at Broad and Green St. (where it ought to be), I lived on the 2700 block of Girard Ave. Across the street from my father's butcher shop was a movie theater, the Elite. We called it the Ee = lite, with the accent on the first syllable. If my homework was done, I was allowed to go to the movies on Tuesday evenings, using the complimentary tickets we received in return for keeping a movie poster in the store window. I remember more vividly, however, Saturday afternoons at the Elite, when all the kids of the neighborhood were there making life miserable for the owner-manager. His name was Sam Stiefel.

"Sonny" Stiefel's path and mine crossed many

years later when he attended Lafayette College and majored in history. As a professor of history at the college, I became his major adviser. He learned of my association with his father and my memories of the Elite. This discovery strengthened the bond between us, and the interest we both had in our Philadelphia backgrounds.

Now, many years later, reading these questions and checking on the answers is an exercise in nostalgia. I only miss a reference to Brewerytown. But this omission is understandable: the great breweries that gave the area its name were all gone by "Sonny" Stiefel's time. Brewerytown might be a good starting point for a second volume of *The Philadelphia Trivia Quiz*.

—Albert W. Gendebien,
Emeritus Professor of History
and College Archivist,
Lafayette College,
Easton, Pa.

Introduction

Although born and raised in Philadelphia, I spent several of my childhood years across the country in Los Angeles. My father moved the family there in 1943, when he was transformed for a few years from a Philadelphia theater owner into a Hollywood producer. But even 3,000 miles away from the watchful eye of Billy Penn, my love for the city never subsided. My heart was always with the Eagles, A's, Phillies, and Penn. My schoolmates knew at all times where my allegiance resided, and a Philadelphia joke might bring a bloodied nose.

In my fierce loyalty to Philadelphia, I followed the excellent example of my father. Whenever he saw a Pennsylvania license plate while driving down Sunset Blvd., he would pull the car over to the curb and find out whether the occupants were from Philly. If so, he would bring them home for lunch or dinner unannounced — a practice my mother did not always find so charming.

So it is with most Philadelphians in exile. No matter where they roam, they retain a loyalty to the city comparable to love of family and country. Talk of the sports teams, the old neighborhood, or the city's favorite foods is common whenever Philadelphians meet on foreign soil. It is hard to explain to an outsider the excitement that Philadelphia inspires among its natives. But it's nearly as hard to convince a Philly native who has never lived anywhere else just what it means to call the Delaware Valley home.

Twice more since that first trip west I have left Philadelphia for educational or career reasons. Now I am once again in exile. But this time it's only 90 miles up the Jersey Turnpike. I can be in my seat at the Vet for a Phils or Eagles game in less than two hours. And if I get a craving, it's not too difficult to take a drive down for a hoagie or a cheese steak or some hardshell crabs at DiNardo's or Walt's.

Living away from the city, and yet close enough to visit regularly, I have watched with pride as Philadelphia has gradually changed its face while managing to hold onto all that made it a great city. This book is my expression of love for all the good things and wonderful people that are my Philadelphia.

—Bernard M. Stiefel

1
Sports

Philadelphia sports fans have suffered more than their share of indignities over the years. The city was long perceived as a haven for losing teams, and its fans were denounced as ill-mannered and unsophisticated. But neither charge has much substance. Philadelphia's sports history boasts a long list of highlights. Only the New York Yankees produced a better record than Connie Mack's A's, and few cities have equaled Philadelphia's contributions to college basketball, boxing, rowing, and track and field. Since the early 1970s, all of the city's major professional teams have been consistent winners, appearing in 11 championship series and winning five major league titles. As for the much-abused Philadelphia sports fan — well, just the sight of hundreds of thousands of people lining Broad Street to welcome home a world champion should speak for itself. Philly sports fans are among the most knowledgeable and sophisticated in America. Even the best, however, may be challenged by some of the following questions on the Philadelphia sports scene.

1. Steve Van Buren, the Eagles star of the late 1940s and early '50s, held many NFL rushing records and was considered possibly the greatest pro running back before the arrival of Cleveland's Jimmy Brown. In college,

Above: The world champion rower of 1947 and '49,
Jack Kelly stands in front of a statue of his equally
famous father. Below: The Eagles celebrate their
1948 NFL championship victory. Steve Van Buren
is holding the ball next to Coach Greasy Neale.

however, he played in the shadow of another running back who went on to achieve fame in a different sport. Name this former L.S.U. All-American.

2. Though restricted from the major leagues for many years, black athletes have made an enormous contribution to Philadelphia professional sports. Name the first black members of the Athletics, Phillies, and Warriors.

3. Bert Bell, former NFL commissioner and Eagles owner, suffered a fatal heart attack while attending one of the team's regular-season games. When and where was the game played, and who was the opposing team?

4. Three NBA players have also played on World Series teams. All three, interestingly, also spent part of their baseball careers with the Phillies. Name them and the World Series teams they played for.

5. Besides Robin Roberts, Curt Simmons, and Jim Konstanty, name at least three pitchers on the Phillies' championship 1950 roster.

6. A member of the 1980 World Champion Phillies was the pitcher who gave up both Ron Santo's first grand slam home run and Jimmy Piersall's 100th homer — the one that occasioned Jimmy's famous run around the bases backward. Who was he?

7. In what year did the Philadelphia Warriors last

win an NBA championship? Who were that team's usual starting five?

8. Name three members of the Philadelphia Flyers who have been NHL trophy winners. What were the trophies, and when did they win them?

9. Although pitcher Curt Simmons played for years in the shadow of teammate Robin Roberts, he did attain a Major League first in the early 1950s. What was it?

10. When was the "Big 5" officially formed? Who won the first title?

11. One father-son combination played for championship Philadelphia teams in the same sport. Name them and the championship teams they played for.

12. Three Phillies managers have returned to the team for a second tour of duty. Name them.

13. Who is the only Phillie ever to win two National League batting titles? What Athletics star won two successive American League batting titles in the 1950s?

14. Who were the Philadelphia Quakers, and what was their dubious distinction?

15. In 1950 an Associated Press poll of sports writers came up with a list of the 10 greatest "20th Century Champions" of sport between

1900 and 1950. The list included such legendary stars as Babe Ruth and Jim Thorpe, along with a native Philadelphian. Who was he?

16. In 1952 Philadelphia was the site for three major championship fights. Jersey Joe Walcott decisioned Ezzard Charles on June 5 to retain the heavyweight title, and was knocked out by Rocky Marciano on September 23 to lose it. What was the third title fight held that year in Philadelphia?

17. On Oct. 20, 1954, Kid Gavilan lost his welterweight title in a Philadelphia bout. Who took it from him?

18. Match the following high school football teams with their nicknames:
    a) Simon Gratz   1) Braves
    b) Northeast   2) Indians
    c) Olney   3) Speedboys
    d) Germantown   4) Rams
    e) Roxborough   5) Vikings
    f) West Philadelphia   6) Trojans
    g) Overbrook   7) Bears
    h) South Philadelphia   8) Bulldogs
    i) John Bartram   9) Hilltoppers

19. Which was the first Philadelphia college basketball team to win a major postseason tournament?

20. With Tom Gola and Norm Grekin leading the way, LaSalle won the 1952 N.I.T. tournament.

Still, its season ended on a sour note when the team lost an important postseason game. What happened?

21. What Penn player won the 1950 Maxwell Football Club award as the outstanding college football player in the country?

22. In 1950, when the Phillies won the National League pennant, who received the "Comeback of the Year" award?

23. Connie Mack spent 50 years as a Major League manager, a record that will probably never be surpassed. How many American League pennants did the A's win under his guidance?
    a) 5
    b) 7
    c) 9
    d) 11

24. Who played third base for the Phillies prior to Mike Schmidt? Who was the Phillies' second baseman in between Dave Cash and Manny Trillo?

25. Despite his .306 average, Richie Ashburn was not the leading hitter for the 1950 pennant-winning Whiz Kids. Who hit better for average that year than Richie?

26. Bill Mlkvy was known as "The Owl Without a Vowel." What fellow Temple star from the same era was called "The Worm."

27. Andy Seminick was traded back to the Phillies by Cincinnati in a six-man deal in 1955. Name at least three other players involved in the trade.

28. Who was the Athletics' last manager in Philadelphia? Who managed them when they moved to Kansas City in 1955?

29. On April 4, 1982, the Phillie Phanatic was given a gala fourth birthday party in front of 25,000 fans at the Vet. The Phanatic's mother was flown in for the event from her home in a remote archipelago. Where was the Phanatic born, and what is his mother's name?

30. Philadelphia's NFL team has been known as the Eagles for every year since 1933 except one. In 1943 the club had a different nickname. What was it, and what were the circumstances?

31. Why is Eagles Coach Marion Campbell known as "The Swamp Fox"?

32. Ownership of the Eagles has changed four times — in 1933, 1949, 1963, and 1969. The 1969 sale price was $16.1 million. How much did the club sell for in 1933?
    a) $4,000
    b) $40,000
    c) $400,000
    d) $4 million

33. In June 1950 Sugar Ray Robinson defeated Robert Villemain of France in a Philadelphia bout to win a disputed title. Explain the circumstances.

34. Since the 76ers arrived from Syracuse in 1963, 12 Big 5 alumni have played for the team. Name at least five, along with their Big 5 schools.

35. This former Philadelphia NBA star was once a world record holder and Olympic gold medalist in track and field. Name him and his event.

36. The Eagles made the 1978 NFL playoffs as the wild card qualifier, ending a long dry spell for the Birds. When was the last previous time they appeared in postseason play?

37. Name the Eagles players or coaches known by the following nicknames:
    a) Bucko
    b) The Hawk
    c) Big Foot
    d) Greasy
    e) The Dutchman
    f) Mr. Automatic
    g) Wild Man
    h) Concrete Charlie
    i) Skippy
    j) Buck

38. On April 18, 1976, in a game against the Chicago Cubs, Mike Schmidt performed a feat that had not been done by a National Leaguer since 1894. What was Schmidt's record-tying achievement?

39. The first Liberty Bowl game was played at Municipal Stadium in 1959, with Penn State beating Alabama 7-0. Name the former Villanova athletic director who founded this bowl game.

40. Tommy Thompson led the Eagles to the NFL championship in 1949, and Norm Van Brocklin did it again in 1960. In between those two great field generals, the Eagles had two regular quarterbacks, who traded the starting role back and forth over a period of several years. Name them.

41. The Eagles' 1960 championship game against Green Bay will long be remembered for Norm Van Brocklin's offensive leadership, Chuck Bednarik's great defensive play, and, of course, Tommy McDonald's touchdown reception and subsequent slide into a snowbank. But whose spectacular play set up the winning Philadelphia touchdown, and who scored it?

42. This Philadelphia native was a football star at North Catholic and Penn, took a shot at minor league baseball for one season, went on to play NFL ball for the New York Giants and the Eagles, and was later football coach and athletic director at Villanova. Name him.

43. On March 2, 1962, Wilt Chamberlain became the only NBA player ever to score 100 points in a game, as the Warriors beat the Knicks 169 to 147. Whose record did Chamberlain break with that incredible performance? Where was the game played?

44. May 31, 1969, is a significant date in Pennsylvania horseracing history. Why?

45. In June 1983 Rusty Staub of the New York Mets tied the Major League record for consecutive pinch hits, when he got eight in a 15-day period. Name the former Phillie whose record he tied.

46. In December 1953 a good Villanova basketball team, with such stars as All-American Bob Schaffer, Larry Tierney, and Jack "Andy" Devine, struggled to win in overtime against a school with a student body of less than 100. Who was this opponent from Ohio, and who was its famous center?

47. Match the following Catholic high school football teams with their nicknames:
    a) West Catholic   1) Cahillites
    b) St. John Neumann   2) Hawklets
    c) Monsignor Bonner   3) Explorers
    d) Roman Catholic   4) Burrs
    e) Northeast Catholic   5) Cardinals
    f) LaSalle   6) Friars
    g) Cardinal Dougherty   7) Falcons
    h) St. Joseph's Prep   8) Pirates

48. Pitcher Rick Wise won 17 games and had a 2.88 ERA for the last-place Phillies in 1971. But he set a Major League record that season, and tied a National League mark, with his hitting. What were his achievements?

49. What five Philadelphia Eagles numbers have been retired, and who wore them?

50. Who was the Eagles coach who also coached a Rose Bowl team and played in a World Series?

51. The 1952 All-Star game played at Shibe Park — the only one ever shortened by rain — featured outstanding performances by two Philadelphia pitchers. The Phils' Curt Simmons pitched three scoreless innings, while the A's' Bobby Shantz, pitching just one inning, struck out three feared hitters on just 13 pitches. Who were the three men he struck out?

52. The 76ers beat the New Jersey Nets by a score of 123-117 on March 23, 1979. The game was unusual for the strange roles played by Harvey Catchings, Eric Money, Ralph Simpson, and Al Skinner. Explain the situation.

53. Before the Fury or the Fever, Philadelphia had a soccer team that represented it in the old American Professional Soccer League. The team was sponsored by a local trucking company. What was the team's name, and where did it play its home games?

54. In the following word find are hidden 50 surnames belonging to professional athletes, coaches, and managers associated with Philadelphia sports. The names may be horizontal, vertical, diagonal, frontwards, backwards, top-to-bottom, or bottom-to-top, and some may overlap others. Some of the names are luminaries in Philadelphia sports history. Others will tax your memory. How many can you find?

```
M Y R R E B S D L U A S S R E G D O R M
O E B R A D L E Y Z Z N O T L R A C O A
S S V S S V Q E E Q T X I O R C A L S H
E P K V S V V R R E T T E B D E L E S G
S M H C U A M T V Z T H G S E W L A O N
G E A B B B T N I E C H G C S D E H V I
D D Y R R O R R N L P O G H O H D C I N
D D D E C C G U G A B B L U R X R I C N
S W A L K E R B S Z P N W L Z E A M H U
S W A S K K E K O N A Z I T I J I R H C
R W O J C I E C H O W I C Z S N G A N H
E A S K U B R A I G O B A E I I S C O A
F L S U L R O L P G B R D N R R Y Y T M
E S A H P Y G B A A F I Q A Q Q A Y S B
O T N A S A N E K F R U N T V J J E N E
H O F R I N I E N B Q E Y N J A N R H R
N N O I R T R X C S L Y L O O E L W O L
R R R C C C M X L E Y L M S S S O J A
O D D H K U H C A R D N I K X Y Z L E I
D G N I N N U B D A L R Y M P L E N N N
```

2
Media

Six years after he arrived in Philadelphia in 1723, Ben Franklin published the first issue of a newspaper called *The Pennsylvania Gazette*. That was the first of Philadelphia's many contributions to the nation's news and entertainment media. The city's newspapers have informed and entertained readers for nearly three centuries; such companies as Curtis Publishing and Triangle Publications have been major forces in magazine publishing; and the Delaware Valley has been the site for numerous firsts in radio and TV broadcasting. The media have also provided Philadelphians with many of their fondest memories of the city — whether it was listening to radio shows produced by the old department-store-owned stations or (for a later generation) being enthralled by Chief Halftown, Sally Starr, and other local TV celebrities. So, as they used to say, return with us now to those thrilling days of yesteryear for some questions on Philadelphia's rich media tradition.

1. Although Dick Clark has been identified with *American Bandstand* for nearly three decades, he was not the program's original host. Who was the first host of *Bandstand*, and who was his sidekick?

Above: The microphones of Philadelphia radio pioneer WCAU record a speech by President Herbert Hoover in 1933. Below: WPEN's 950 Club, with Joe Grady (left) and Ed Hurst, was one of the most popular local shows of the 1950s.

2. The only live Western series to appear on network TV originated from what is now the parking lot behind WCAU-TV. Name the show.

3. Before the *Today* show premiered in 1952, WPTZ-TV broadcast a popular local morning show in the 7-9 a.m. time slot. Who were the show's hosts?

4. Who was the host of *Horn & Hardart's Children's Hour*? Name three prominent entertainers whose careers began on this popular Sunday show.

5. What 69th St. appliance dealer, accompanied by his dog, did his own commercials on a Sunday-evening TV show sponsored by his store in the 1950s? What was the show called?

6. Who did the early-evening sportscasts for WFIL-TV for most of the 1950s, and what was his nightly sports segment called? Who handled the sports on WFIL radio for most of this period?

7. WIP's *Dawn Patrol* was an after-midnight staple on Philadelphia radio from the 1940s through the '60s. What record was played at least once every night on the show, and who was the program's longest-running D.J.? By what method did listeners make requests?

8. Name at least three national magazines once published by the Curtis Publishing Co.

9. Name at least five ethnic newspapers published in the Philadelphia area.

10. On January 10, 1970, a group of youths invaded the WCAU-TV studios at City Line and Monument Road, smashing windows and cutting phone lines before being arrested. They were protesting a program that had recently aired on CBS-TV. What was the show?

11. Who was the voice of Penn football on WCAU radio during the 1950s? Who broadcast the Quakers' games when they were on WFIL? Who broadcast the Villanova games around the same time?

12. The 1975 Pulitzer Prize for national reporting went to two Philadelphia reporters. Who were they, and why did they win it?

13. The call letters for WIBG and WJMJ had religious significance when originally chosen. What did they stand for?

14. Next to *Bandstand*, the most popular local teenage music show of the late 1950s was WPEN's *950 Club*, hosted by Joe Grady and Ed Hurst. What musical instrument did Grady play on the show? What did Ed call Joe on the show, and what did Joe call Ed?

15. Established in the late 1960s, this Philadelphia FM station was one of the nation's first to succeed with a 24-hour format of album rock. Name this "grand old man" of FM rock.

16. Can you match the following radio stations with their spot on the dial?

    a) WYSD-FM   1) 1480
    b) WIBG   2) 98.1
    c) WFIL   3) 1210
    d) WDAS   4) 610
    e) WHAT   5) 94.1
    f) WCAU-FM   6) 106.1
    g) WIP   7) 990
    h) WWSH-FM   8) 95.7
    i) KYW   9) 1340
    j) WCAU   10) 560
    k) WMMR-FM   11) 96.5
    l) WFLN-FM   12) 950
    m) WWDB-FM   13) 1540
    n) WRCP   14) 93.3
    o) WPEN   15) 1060

17. In 1974 a conservative clergyman from Media who owned an FM radio station was denied renewal of his FCC license because he failed to give time to alternative views. Who was he?

18. In 1953 the Philco Corp. sold WPTZ-TV/Channel 3 to Westinghouse Broadcasting. The event set the stage for an elaborate celebration and TV special. Why was the event considered significant in broadcasting circles?

19. Besides WPTZ, name two other sets of call letters that Channel 3 has used since the early 1950s.

20. Alan Arkin starred in a 1978 TV movie on CBS called *The Other Side of Hell*. What was the movie's connection with Philadelphia?

21. What was the TV "first" that took place in April 1949 at the old Roosevelt Theater on Frankford Ave.?

22. *TV Guide* magazine, based in Radnor, is one of the nation's most successful publications. The national magazine, however, evolved from a local publication that preceded it. What was this local magazine called, and when did it start?

23. Chief Halftown has entertained and counseled a couple of generations of Philadelphia children on TV. What is the chief's full name? What were the Seneca Indian words he spoke to open and close his show?

24. In 1954 an Army PFC got his own Saturday-night TV show on Channel 6. His musical talents drew many Philadelphia viewers away from such popular network fare as Ted Mack's *Original Amateur Hour* and *The Jackie Gleason Show*. Who was this soldier, and what was the name of his show?

25. Puppeteer Lee Dexter had a successful Sunday-morning children's show on Channel 3 for many years. What was the name of the show's "star," and who was his sidekick?

26. At 12:15 every weekday afternoon, Acme Markets used to invite Philadelphians of all ages to lunch on Channel 3 with a nice man who sketched, showed old movies, and chatted with a squirrel. Who was the host, what was the show called, and what was the squirrel's name?

27. Weather people began appearing on Phila-
    delphia TV during the 1950s, and many of them
    remained local personalities well into the 1960s
    and '70s. Match the following weathercaster
    with his or her station:
    a) Francis Davis   1) Channel 3
    b) Lyn Dollar   2) Channel 6
    c) Phil Sheridan   3) Channel 10

28. This local sports commentator, best known for
    his weeknight *Sports Final* on Channel 10 in
    the 1950s, went on to a successful network
    career. Name him.

29. All of the following were local quiz or
    audience-participation shows once seen on
    Philadelphia TV. Can you name their hosts?
    a) *Cinderella Weekend*
    b) *Fun and Fortune*
    c) *Movie Quick Quiz*
    d) *Nose for the News*
    e) *Stop, Look & Listen*
    f) *Shop 'n' Sing*
    g) *Mystery Star Quiz*

30. Though most Philadelphia radio stations are
    now located on City Line or in Roxborough,
    many were formerly located in Center City.
    Match the stations with their old addresses.
    a) WFIL   1) 1425 Walnut
    b) WIP   2) 1622 Chestnut
    c) WPEN   3) Widener Bldg.
    d) WIBG   4) 35 South 9th St.
    e) KYW   5) 1211 Chestnut
    f) WCAU   6) 1619 Walnut

g) WDAS   7) Ledger Bldg.
h) WHAT   8) 1528 Walnut

31. One of WIP radio's most popular daytime shows was hosted by "Tiny" Ruffner and Johnny Wilcox and featured visits to area shopping centers, where prizes were awarded to quiz contestants. Name the show.

32. *The Big Top* was a popular Philadelphia show for many years, bringing viewers, as well as a studio audience seated around its one ring, the best in circus acts. Who was the show's ringmaster, and what Philadelphia TV personality played one of the two featured clowns?

33. One of Philadelphia's most popular sportswriters used a name identified with the sport he covered. Who was he?

34. Sally Starr, who appeared for many years on Channel 6, was Philadelphia's favorite TV cowgirl. In real life she was married to another TV cowperson. Can you name him?

35. Don Curtis was the host for *TV Thriller*, which appeared on Channel 3 every Saturday night from 11 to midnight during much of the 1950s. What was the beer that sponsored the show?

36. Bill Sears's show *In the Park* featured the puppets of the husband-wife team of Paul Ritts and Mary Holliday. What were the names of the ostrich and the chipmunk that appeared on the show?

37. Before he became a nationally known comedian, David Brenner worked as a writer for a Philadelphia radio station. Name the station.

38. What Philadelphia car company has long billed itself in radio commercials as "The World's Smallest Chevrolet Dealer"? Which dealer was once known as "The Chevrolet Tycoon"?

39. Who was the handicapped actress who starred in Philadelphia's first local TV soap opera? What was the name of the show?

40. What do the call letters WPVI stand for?

41. Former Deputy Mayor Al Gaudioso is best known for his political activities. But what media job did he once hold, and what was his most famous achievement in that job?

42. Who was TV's "Miss Terry," and why did her career end at an early age?

43. In the early 1950s Ed McMahon was a jack-of-all-trades for Channel 10, hosting various shows, appearing as a clown on *The Big Top*, and co-hosting a weekday-morning show with Don Prindle, seen at 9:15. What was the show called? Name three of its regular performers.

44. Considered one of the nation's finest storytellers, this man was heard on New York's WOR radio for more than 25 years. Before that he was a regular on KYW, where he first used the *Bahn Frei Polka*, by Eduard Strauss, as his

theme song. Who is this well-known radio personality and writer?

45. Humorist Henry Morgan was once a staff announcer at WCAU radio. What was the gag he pulled that reportedly caused his premature departure from the station?

46. What local radio personality referred to himself as "opinionated but lovable"? Which one nicknamed his regular listeners, "Pyle drivers"?

47. Identify the hosts of the following local TV shows geared toward the 1950s housewife:
    a) *Carol Calling*
    b) *The Girl Next Door*
    c) *Pots, Pans and Personalities*

48. This local radio personality held down simultaneous jobs at two stations by interchanging his first and last names. What were his two names?

49. The Phillies broadcasting booth has long been stocked with some of the best talent in the major leagues. Name the three main announcers who did Phillies play-by-play during the 1950s and '60s.

3
Entertainment, Recreation, and Dining

Philadelphia today is a dining and entertainment delight, with a multitude of excellent restaurants, trendy discos, theaters, and dance companies, as well as one of the nation's leading symphony orchestras. But entertainment is another area where Philadelphians have sometimes labored under an inferiority complex. Whether because of the infamous "blue laws," a rather drab Center City, or the proximity to New York, the city did lack some excitement in the old days. We all spent a lot of Saturday nights over in Jersey — and that wasn't so hot either. But the situation was never as bleak as fable has it. Even in its less "enlightened" days, Philadelphia had several successful night clubs, vaudeville houses, and legitimate theaters, some of which are all but forgotten today. As you go through the questions that follow, you may recall that Philadelphia wasn't quite the sleepy town it was reputed to be.

*Philadelphians queue up in front of the old Er-
langer Theater, one of Center City's many now-defunct movie and stage palaces.*

1. Where was the Latin Casino located before it moved to Cherry Hill? What is currently on the site?

2. A popular lightweight boxer of the 1920s later owned a Center City restaurant that bore his name. The night spot was also the site of two radio talk shows on WPEN. Who was the restaurateur, and what were the radio shows?

3. From the 1920s until the '70s, many black performers got their start on the old "black circuit" of vaudeville houses in such cities as Philadelphia, New York, Baltimore, Washington, and Chicago. Name four prominent black vaudeville houses in Philadelphia during those years. Which one still stands?

4. Philadelphia's Walnut Street Theater, opened in 1809, is the oldest theater in continual use in the United States. Originally, however, it was known by a different name. What was it called, and what were its main attractions?

5. The Academy of Music was modeled after what famous European structure? By what nickname has it been known throughout the years?

6. Woodside Park was the city's major amusement park through most of the 20th century. Where was the park located, and what were its two roller coasters called?

7. At what famous Philadelphia restaurant during the 1940s could a diner have his tea leaves read?

8. Palumbo's, at 8th and Catharine, is a favorite South Philly gathering place, but owner Frank Palumbo had another popular club during the 1940s at 6th and Market. Name it.

9. Three of Philadelphia's four major night clubs in the 1950s — Palumbo's, the Latin Casino, and the Celebrity Room — were located south of Market Street. Name the fourth, located at 5th and Pike.

10. Who was hostess and main attraction of the Celebrity Room?

11. America's first automat opened in Philadelphia in 1902. Where was it located, and when did it finally close?

12. What was *Stars on Ice*, and where was it located?

13. Who was the "King of Shrimps"?

14. In the 1950s, this exotic dancer was the much-publicized main attraction at The Wedge, a night spot at Broad and Ridge. Who was she, and what was the name of her dance?

15. Siegmund "Pop" Lubin had an optical store on Arch St. near 9th around the turn of the century. What was this Jewish immigrant's claim to fame?

16. Match the following night spots, favorite rendezvous places for teenagers in the 1950s

and '60s, with the town or area in which they were located:

a) Don's   1) Yeadon
b) Hawaiian Cottage   2) Broad & Locust
c) The Pub   3) Broad & Steton
d) The Hot Shoppe   4) Cherry Hill, N.J.
e) The Harvey House   5) Airport Circle,
                                   Camden, N.J.

17. Among its many achievements, the Philadelphia Orchestra was the first symphony orchestra to appear on a sponsored radio broadcast (October 6, 1929), and the first to appear on television (March 20, 1948). It was also the first to appear in a movie. What was this 1938 film?

18. The Horn & Hardart automats featured coin slots and little glass windows. How did Linton's deliver the food?

19. What was the last feature shown at the old Stanley Theater?

20. Match the following Philadelphia jazz spots with their onetime locations:

a) The Showboat   1) Broad & South
b) The Blue Note   2) Broad & Lombard
c) Billy Krechmer's   3) 13th & Ridge
d) Pep's Show Bar   4) 16th & Ranstead

21. Like New York's famous Circle Line, Philadelphia once had a cruise line that toured the Delaware River. Name it.

22. Where would you find the Thunderbolt, Bluebeard's Castle, and the Alps?

23. Match the following now-defunct movie theaters with their locations:

a) Boyd	1) 52nd and Market
b) Victoria	2) 16th and Market
c) Erlanger	3) 19th and Chestnut
d) Midway	4) Frankford and Allegheny
e) Earle	5) 21st and Market
f) Fox	6) 20th and Market
g) Nixon	7) 11th and Market
h) Allegheny	8) Allegheny & Kensington
i) Mastbaum	9) 9th and Market
j) Karlton	10) 8th and Market
k) Arcadia	11) 12th and Market
l) Capitol	12) 16th and Chestnut
m) Palace	13) 52nd and Chestnut
n) State	14) Broad and Chestnut

24. Before Sunday drinking was legalized, private clubs flourished in Philadelphia as places where members could drink past midnight on Saturday night. Most of the biggest clubs, like the Alpha and the RDA, were located in Center City, but a major club in the northeast competed for the leading night-club talent of the day. Name it.

25. What did Tempest Storm, Carrie Fennell, and Georgia Southern have in common?

26. Name the five best-known seafood restaurants in Atlantic City during its heyday.

27. Name the two most famous brands of Atlantic City salt water taffy.

28. What famous movie couple of the 1930s and

'40s began singing together at the original Robin Hood Dell, with the Philadelphia Orchestra in the pit?

29. What cartoon character once helped Leopold Stokowski conduct the Philadelphia Orchestra?

30. Bert Parks was, of course, the longest-running host of the Miss America pageant. But who was the singing emcee who immediately preceded him?

31. The Philadelphia Zoo is considered one of the finest in the world. One of its major attractions for years has been a gorilla that was born at the zoo and is currently the oldest gorilla in captivity. Who is this hometown boy?

32. A prominent Philadelphia performing arts organization, along with a world-famous performer, sponsored an international voice competition in 1980-81, which featured 500 singers from 33 countries. What was the organization, and who was the performer?

33. Philadelphia is well known for such food specialties as the soft pretzel, the hoagie, and the cheese steak. What South Philadelphia eatery is credited with introducing the hot dog roll back in 1895?

34. Name the hotels that housed the following rooms for dining and entertainment:
a) Kite and Key
b) Coach Room

c) Hunt Room
d) Persian Room
e) Hamilton Room
f) Salubra Room

35. The Troc was the last of the city's great burlesque houses. What is the theater currently being used for? Name two other theaters specializing in burlesque that were once located at 40th and Market and at Germantown and Allegheny.

36. What was the first city-owned, operated and managed theater in the United States?

37. When the Arena went up in smoke in the fall of 1983, an era in Philadelphia entertainment and sports ended. The "old barn" officially opened on February 14, 1920, with an ice hockey match between Yale and Princeton. What was the original name of the building?

38. Located for more than 60 years at 17th and Delancey Place, Plays and Players is the oldest amateur theatrical organization in the country. One of its most famous productions was a 1948 play that went on to become a prize-winning Broadway hit and later a movie starring William Holden. Name the play.

39. In the 1970s Resorts International bought two of Atlantic City's most famous pieces of real estate. One was the hotel that now bears its name. The other was the famous Steel Pier. Do you remember:

a) the former name of the hotel?

b) the name of the family that owned and operated the Steel Pier for many years?

c) the main attraction at the end of the pier and the permanent exhibit at its entrance on the Boardwalk?

40. *Rocky* was not the only Hollywood movie filmed in Philadelphia. Match the following films made in the area with their male stars:

a) *Outside the Walls* (1950)   1) Dan Duryea

b) *The Burglar* (1957)   2) George Segal

c) *The Last Man* (1969)   3) Richard Basehart

d) *King of Marvin Gardens* (1972)   4) Alan Arkin

e) *Last of the Red Hot Lovers* (1972)   5) Jack Nicholson

f) *A Touch of Class* (1973)   6) Sidney Poitier

41. This late Hollywood leading man made his movie debut in a 1958 horror movie filmed in Philadelphia. Name the movie and the star.

42. The first play written by a black to win a Drama Critics Circle Award opened in Philadelphia at the Walnut Street Theater on January 26, 1959. What was the play?

43. The Stanley Theater was one of Philadelphia's most famous film houses. For whom was it named?

44. The horses that pulled the wagons were dappled gray and stood at least 16 hands high. The little girl on the logo was named Mary Jane. These delicacies were first manufactured in an old foundry building near the newly completed Shibe Park. Name this famous dessert.

45. The Savoy Company, a frequent attraction at the Academy of Music and Longwood Gardens in Kennett Square, was founded in Philadelphia in 1901. What is its historical claim to fame?

46. What was the first all-talking motion picture to play in Philadelphia, and where was it shown?

47. This quaint form of transportation, introduced in 1887, was first used by invalids and later became fashionable among the well-to-do. It totally disappeared in 1974, but is now enjoying something of a revival. It was even included in New Jersey's exhibit at the 1964 World's Fair in New York City. What was it?

48. The South Jersey seashore has served as a restful retreat for millions of people over the years. It was also once the site of the summer White House. Who was the President who relaxed at "the Shore"?

49. Philadelphian Pearl Bailey was discovered on amateur night at the old Pearl Theater at 21st and Ridge. Though less well remembered today, her brother, Bill, was also discovered there. What was his talent?

4
Places and Landmarks

Do you really think you know Philadelphia and the Delaware Valley? Maybe you know what it looks like today, but can you remember what Center City, South Street, Society Hill, Queen Village, and University City looked like before the renovation boom of the 1970s? Few places have been as successful as Philadelphia in blending the new with the old, modernizing itself while maintaining and restoring its treasured past. Living in the city, many Philadelphians often overlook what is just under their nose. The questions in this chapter test your knowledge of the physical city and its environs, along with its many landmarks, both present and past.

1. What were the former names of JFK Stadium and JFK Boulevard?

2. Where was the Chinese Wall, and what purpose did it serve?

Above: The Philadelphia Museum of Art is one of the city's most prestigious cultural institutions. Below: Looking up the Delaware in 1957.

3. The Hershey Hotel in Center City occupies the site where another elegant hotel once stood. By what two names was that hotel known, and what famous night spot was located atop the building?

4. Why is the area from Merion to Paoli known as the Main Line?

5. If someone told you to "meet me at the eagle," where would you go?

6. What is commemorated by the fire that burns at the center of Washington Park?

7. What was the former name of Philadelphia International Airport?

8. What major hotels once stood at the following locations?
   a) 13th and Filbert
   b) Broad and Walnut (SE corner)
   c) Chestnut at 13th
   d) 39th and Chestnut (SW corner)
   e) 10th and Walnut
   f) 36th and Chestnut
   g) Locust St. off Broad

9. What significance does the following sequence of numbers have for Philadelphians: 2, 5, 8, 11, 13, 15, 32, 36, 40, 46, 52, 60, 63, and 69?

10. A statue is located directly across from the main branch of the Philadelphia Free Library. To whom is it dedicated, and what is the quotation inscribed on it?

11. The Platt Bridge, the principal route across the Schuylkill River to Philadelphia International Airport, was known for many years as the Penrose Bridge. Who was Penrose?

12. For whom is Reyburn Plaza named?

13. What distinction does Philadelphia hold as a port?

14. One word very important to Philadelphians is misspelled on the Liberty Bell. What is it?

15. Seven out of ten Philadelphians have never visited the Liberty Bell, but see if you can match the following Philadelphia historical landmarks with their proper location:

a) Betsy Ross House	1) Chestnut below 4th
b) First Bank of the U.S.	2) 5th and Arch
c) Edgar Allen Poe House	3) Swanson near Front and Christian
d) Gloria Dei (old Swede's Church)	4) 239 Arch
e) Elfreth's Alley	5) 244 S. 3rd
f) Carpenter's Hall	6) 7th & Brandywine
g) Christ Church Cemetery	7) Arch between Front and 2nd
h) Powell House	8) 116 S. 3rd
i) Mikveh Israel Cemetery	9) 419 S. 6th
j) Mother Bethel A.M.E. Church	10) Spruce near 8th

16. The Rodin Museum on Ben Franklin Parkway at 22nd houses the largest collection of the sculptor's works outside of the Musee Rodin in Paris. Who donated the museum to the city?

17. Although it occupies less area than Los Angeles's Griffith Park or Cleveland's Emerald Necklace, Fairmount Park still ranks as the largest municipal landscaped park in the United States. Why?

18. Where is the only covered bridge in Philadelphia?

19. On November 3, 1967, the wrecking ball began to demolish a 132-year-old structure at 10th and Dickinson to make way for a neighborhood park. What was the building?

20. On April 23, 1952, the Philadelphia Orchestra played a command performance to say farewell to another Philadelphia landmark. What was it?

21. What famous establishment on South 9th St. closed its doors for the last time in November 1968?

22. Name four major ethnic museums located in Philadelphia.

23. What were Philadelphia's five original squares — both their original names and the names by which they are known today?

24. Name the eight counties that comprise metro-politan Philadelphia.

25. On April 20, 1969, a famous symbol was taken down from Building 17 at the RCA facility in Camden. What was it?

26. If you stand at just the right spot in the Phila-delphia Museum of Art and look down the Parkway toward City Hall, you can see the work of three generations of a famous artistic family. What family?

27. Who is honored by the statue in McPherson Square at Kensington and Indiana avenues?

28. Where can you find Grace Kelly's wedding dress and her father's racing shell from the 1920 Olympics?

29. There is something unusual about the numerals on the face of the Independence Hall Tower clock. What is it?

30. The nation's first stone bridge is located in the Philadelphia area. Where is it?

31. New York has Grant's Tomb. What structure in Fairmount Park is also associated with the former President and Civil War general?

32. The area between 8th and 11th on Market St. once housed most of the city's leading depart-ment stores. Name four that no longer exist.

33. Boat House Row on East River Drive has long been a key part of Philadelphia's social scene. By what nickname have the rowing clubs there long been known?

34. Tun Tavern, which once stood at the intersection of Front, Water, and King streets, was the site of the founding of a major military organization. What was it?

35. What Philadelphia church claims the distinction of being the oldest continuously operated black church in America?

36. During the 1930s, '40s, and '50s, Philadelphia had a number of local boxing clubs and other buildings where big matches were staged. Which of the following was *not* part of the Philadelphia boxing scene in those years?
    a) Toppi Stadium
    b) The Met
    c) The Cambria
    d) The Pla-Mor
    e) The Adelphia
    f) Blue Horizon Ballroom

37. The face of Atlantic City has undergone a dramatic change, but the memory of its many grand old hotels lingers on. Can you name ten of them?

38. Philadelphia is the only city in the United States where you can view a real saint. Who and where?

39. Gloucester County is one of the most rural and least-developed of the counties that make up the greater Philadelphia area. Which of the following towns is *not* located in Gloucester County?
    a) Woodbury
    b) Gloucester
    c) Swedesboro
    d) Pitman
    e) Paulsboro
    f) Glassboro

40. What South Jersey shore town has for years been a favorite summer retreat for Philadelphia politicians and is often referred to as "The Irish Riviera"?

41. The nation's longest trolley route is located in Philadelphia. Which route is it?

42. This Philadelphia neighborhood was reputedly given its nickname by Charles Dickens on a visit to the city in 1842. Name the area.

43. How did the Overbrook section supposedly get its name?

44. One major Philadelphia street has a name derived from two Lenape Indian words that literally mean "place of pigeon droppings." Name this unfortunate street.

45. The Pennsylvania Academy of the Fine Arts, at Broad and Cherry, is one of the city's most

notable artistic institutions. It also holds a national distinction. What is its claim to fame?

46. The Benjamin Franklin Parkway was modeled after a famous European thoroughfare. Name it.

47. Despite angry opposition from residents of Lower Merion and Haverford townships, this service was discontinued in 1966 after more than 60 years of operation. Name it.

5.
People, Events, and Potpourri

Though Philadelphia is frequently overshadowed by its two more high-profile neighbors on the Eastern Seaboard, New York and Washington, the city has an amazingly rich and varied history of its own. Presidents have been nominated and great ships have been launched here. There have been major disasters, elaborate celebrations, and stirring moments of patriotic significance. But more than great events, Philadelphia is the home of great people. People from Fishtown, Bala-Cynwyd, and South Philly; from Chestnut Hill, Upper Darby, and Chester. People who teach at Haverford, and sell produce in the Italian Market. People who speak Chinese, Polish, Lebanese, and Yiddish. Most of all, people who love their city. Test yourself on these questions about some of the best-known people and events in Philadelphia's recent past.

1. In what neighborhood did Bill Cosby, one of Philadelphia's most famous natives, grow up? What college did he attend, and what sport did he play there?

Above: City Councilman Thatcher Longstreth tries to show Mike Schmidt a thing or two. Below: An autogiro, invented by Pitcairn Aviation Co., hovers over Center City in 1930.

2. Al Capone was arrested only three times in his life. One was for tax evasion, one was for failure to testify in court, and the other was for an offense committed while traveling through Philadelphia. What was the charge, and where was he held?

3. What does the word Philadelphia mean? What is the official motto of the city, as it appears on the seal of the city, and what does it mean?

4. What do these three Philadelphia beauties have in common: Frances Marie Burke, Ruth Malcolmson, and Rose Coyle?

5. What major U.S. airline had its origins in Philadelphia?

6. Twice in 1968 — on February 23 and again on March 1 — high winds caused some controversial damage in Philadelphia. What happened?

7. What was the last national political convention to be held in Philadelphia? What was the last political convention in Philadelphia to nominate a man who eventually won the presidency?

8. President Gerald Ford and Jimmy Carter held a debate in Philadelphia during their 1976 campaign for the presidency. Where was it held?

9. What was the inspiration for Elton John's 1974 hit song *Philadelphia Freedom*?

10. What famous Philadelphia singer had a park named after him?

11. The 1958 statewide elections were nearly a complete sweep for the Democrats. But Hugh D. Scott, Jr., a Republican from Philadelphia, bucked the trend as he defeated a Democratic opponent for U.S. senator. Who was the losing Democrat?

12. In May 1958 Pat Nixon, wife of then-Vice President Richard Nixon, came to Camden to perform what honorary function?

13. In 1956 the Pennsylvania and New Jersey turnpikes were officially linked, as their common bridge over the Delaware was completed. Name the two governors who presided over the dedication ceremony.

14. These annual campus high jinks were a tradition on the Penn campus every spring until May 3, 1956, when the fun turned into a five-hour riot, in which two policemen were injured and 117 students arrested. What was the name of these events?

15. In April 1956 Mrs. Matthew H. McCloskey of Philadelphia had $45,000 worth of jewelry stolen from her hotel room in Europe. Where was she, and why was she there?

16. Since Joseph Clark's election in 1951, Democrats have dominated the office of Philadelphia mayor. Name the Republican

candidates who lost to each of the following
victorious Democrats:
a) Clark (1951)
b) Richardson Dilworth (1955)
c) Dilworth (1959)
d) James Tate (1963)
e) Tate (1967)
f) Frank Rizzo (1971)
g) Rizzo (1975)
h) William Green (1979)
i) Wilson Goode (1983)

17. What was "Operation Scram"?

18. Two major explosions rocked Philadelphia
within a month of each other in the spring of
1956. What were they?

19. This man withdrew as a Democratic candidate
for the U.S. Senate in 1956, opening the way
for Joseph Clark to run for the seat and eventually win it. Who was he?

20. One day after Mayor Joseph Clark took the
oath of office on January 7, 1952, another
well-known Philadelphia leader took over a
high position. Who was he?

21. The following native Philadelphians have
achieved greater fame by other names. Who
are they?
a) Ernest Evans
b) William Claude Dukenfield
c) Elaine Berlin
d) Alfredo Cocozza

e) Myrtle Swoyer

22. The largest single employer in North Philadelphia is also the sixth largest in the entire city. Name it.

23. Jack Rosenberg was born in Jefferson Hospital on September 5, 1935. He lived in an apartment at Bala Ave. and City Line until he was 15 and graduated from Norristown High School. By what name is Jack Rosenberg better known?

24. What former president of the University of Pennsylvania has run for President of the United States?

25. Mayor Frank Rizzo once raised a ruckus by threatening to sue a company that had sprayed a chemical on his lawn, which he claimed was harmful to his dog. What was the dog's name?

26. From 1936 until the 1960s, the northwest corner of 10th and Chestnut was dominated by one person. Who?

27. On April 14, 1966, a unique event in Philadelphia history took place at the Arena. It was viewed by Judge Edward J. Griffiths, who made a ruling about it the following day. What was the event, and how did Judge Griffiths rule?

28. James Tate became mayor of Philadelphia in February 1962 without being elected to the post. How did he become mayor?

29. What was the Sabbatorian Relief Bill?

30. Who was Dexter, and why was his death in 1968 significant?

31. In 1967 two of the world's most powerful leaders got together at an area campus for some important discussions. Who were the leaders, where did they hold their meeting, and why was the site chosen?

32. This movie and TV star called President Johnson an S.O.B. at a public rally that opened Sen. Eugene McCarthy's campaign headquarters in Philadelphia in April 1968. Who was he?

33. A landmark U.S. Supreme Court decision on May 20, 1968, ended a 140-year fight over a man's will and the racial makeup of a Philadelphia institution. What was this decision?

34. On June 8, 1968, thousands of Philadelphians lined the tracks at the 30th Street and North Philadelphia stations to view a special train as it made its way through the area. What was this train?

35. What happened to Susan Davis and Elizabeth Perry on Memorial Day weekend in 1969 that remains of concern to residents of the Ocean City area?

36. According to popular legend, the inscription on W.C. Fields's grave reads: "I'd rather be here than in Philadelphia." Actually, the inscription

merely says: "W.C. Fields 1880-1946." How did the misconception originate?

37. What is the Guardian Civic League, and what did it give to Charles Evers, then mayor of Fayette, Miss., at a dinner in his honor in November 1969?

38. What is the connection between the Mikveh Israel Cemetery and the novel *Ivanhoe*?

39. The Mummers Parade has become a New Year's Day tradition in Philadelphia. When was the first one held?

40. On February 6, 1970, Captain Clarence C. Ferguson retired. Who was he, and what record does he hold?

41. What Philadelphian was the first American artist ever to be honored by a dinner in the White House?

42. James Buchanan, a native of Lancaster who became the nation's 15th President, is the closest Philadelphia has ever come to having a native son as chief executive. But one Philadelphian did make Vice President. A city in Texas was later named for him. Who was he?

43. The Pep Boys were Manny, Moe, and Jack. What were their last names? Which one left Philadelphia to start another business, and what was the business?

44. At the beginning of 1984 the starting salary for a Philadelphia police officer was $19,936. How much was it in 1965?
    a) $4,236
    b) $6,101
    c) $8,807
    d) $9,622

45. SEPTA, the Southeast Pennsylvania Transit Authority, took over for the old P.T.C. (Philadelphia Transit Company). What did P.T.C. succeed?

46. Who was the Philadelphian who commanded the Army Air Force in World War II and later had a suburban high school football field named for him?

47. The world's first large-scale electronic digital computer was developed in the mid-1940s at the University of Pennsylvania's Moore School of Electrical Engineering. What was the acronym for this important breakthrough?

48. Who was the victim of the "snow shovel killer" in Atlantic City during the winter of 1978?

49. Even before deregulation of the banking industry and the recent wave of mergers, many well-known Philadelphia banking institutions were bought out by larger banks. Each of the now-defunct banks on the left was taken over by one of the Philadelphia financial institutions on the right. Can you match them?

a) Corn Exchange

b) Land Title Bank & Trust

c) Liberty Real Estate Bank & Trust

d) Delaware County Trust

e) Market Street National Bank

f) First National Bank of Conshohocken

g) Second National Bank

h) Trademan's National Bank

i) Ninth Bank & Trust

1) Provident National Bank

2) Philadelphia National Bank

3) Fidelity Bank

4) Girard Bank

50. In Philadelphia, as in other U.S. cities, telephone exchanges once had names and not just numbers. Can you remember the names that went with the following exchanges?

a) 23 (BE)

b) 24 (CH)

c) 54 (KI)

d) 62 (MA)

e) 73 (PE)

f) 43 (GE)

g) 38 (EV)

h) 84 (VI)

i) 87 (TR)

j) 67 (OR)

k) 53 (JE)

l) 46 (HO)

6.
Guest Shots

Everyone who lives in Philadelphia has his or her own store of trivia, so it only seems fair to give at least a few of them equal time. On the pages that follow, some of the people who have helped make Philadelphia so interesting have contributed their own favorite trivia questions about the city we all love.

1. *Thomas Foglietta, U.S. congressman, 1st District:*
   Many of us have stories or bits of knowledge about our City Hall. But would you know where to go if I asked you to meet me at its main entrance?

2. *Wilson Goode, mayor:*
   Only one building in Philadelphia remains standing from the 1876 Centennial Exposition. What is the building, where is it located, and what is it still used for?

3. *Joe Frazier, former heavyweight champion of the world:*
   At the Olympic qualification fights in 1964, I was defeated in one bout, but my opponent

Above: Mayor Wilson Goode (right) and his predecessor, William Green. Below: Former Eagles star Tommy McDonald and WCAU broadcaster Steve Fredericks.

broke his wrist and I went to the Olympics in his place. Who was the fighter who beat me, and what was ironic about my later winning of the gold medal?

4. *Thatcher Longstreth, city councilman and former Republican candidate for mayor:*
   The Metropolitan Hospital at 8th and Race St. is built on the site of an old-time entertainment palace. Name it.

5. *Clark DeLeon,* Philadelphia Inquirer *staff writer:*
   Publisher J. David Stein folded his crusading liberal newspaper the *Philadelphia Record* in 1947 because of a strike by the Newspaper Guild. Why was his action ironic?

6. *Dr. Constance Clayton, superintendent of schools for the city of Philadelphia.*
   Can you name the last five people who served as superintendent of Philadelphia schools?

7. *Dick Vermeil, CBS-TV sports analyst and former Eagles coach:*
   The Eagles clinched their first playoff position in nearly two decades in the last game of the 1978 season. Who was the opposing team that day, who scored the Eagles' final touchdown, and what was the final score?

8. *Bill Hart, WCAU-AM broadcaster:*
   Name three Philadelphia professional athletes who played with only one eye.

9. *Frank Rizzo, former mayor and police com-*

missioner:

Many nicknames were tagged on me when I was with the Philadelphia police department. The most lasting one was first shouted at me while I was chasing an armed man at 4th and Montrose St. in 1950. What was it?

10. *Albert Taxin, Old Original Bookbinder's, 125 Walnut St.:*

The President's Room at Old Original Bookbinder's displays a portrait of every President of the United States, along with one "outsider." Who else is pictured there?

11. *Jack McKinney, Philadelphia Daily News columnist:*

Although she achieved most of her success in Hollywood movies, Philadelphian Jeanette MacDonald once appeared on a Philadelphia stage in a rare venture into another form of entertainment. What was it?

12. *John Facenda, the late radio and TV newscaster:*

Zack Clayton is best known as the former chairman of the Pennsylvania State Athletic Commission and one of the leading boxing referees in the world. But he first gained recognition as a star player in another sport. Can you name the sport, and the famous team he played for?

13. *Frank Olivieri, Pat's King of Steaks, 9th and Wharton St.:*

In 1952 a major Hollywood movie was shot on the land where Veterans Stadium now stands. What was the movie?

14. *Chuck Stone,* Philadelphia Daily News *senior editor:*
Only three female Republicans have been elected to the state legislature since 1940. Name them.

15. *Jack Kelly, business executive and former city councilman:*
Name at least five Olympic gold medal winners from Philadelphia.

16. *Gene Crane, WCAU station announcer:*
For a time in the early 1950s, more network TV shows originated from Philadelphia than from Hollywood. Can you name at least five of these locally produced shows?

17. *Marge Tartaglione, chairwoman of the City Commission:*
In 1965 Philadelphians elected a registered Democrat to the office of District Attorney on a Republican ticket. Who was he?

18. *Carl Peterson, general manager of the Philadelphia Stars:*
The Stars' head coach, Jim Mora, played tight end and defensive end at Occidental College in California. Who was the quarterback for that team?

19. *Sam and Richard Bookbinder, Bookbinder's Seafood House, 215 South 15th St.*
When did it finally become legal for Pennsylvanians to buy a drink in a public place on Sun-

day? When was the first legal Sunday drink in Philadelphia actually taken?

20. *William Green, attorney and former mayor:*
What were the Eagles' original team colors before the current green and white? Why did the team choose the eagle as its symbol?

21. *Leonard Tose, owner and president of the Philadelphia Eagles:*
Besides Tom Brookshier and Irv Cross, name one other current CBS sportscaster who was originally drafted by the Eagles.

22. *Edgar Williams,* Philadelphia Inquirer *columnist:*
Most Philadelphians remember JFK Stadium when it was known as Municipal Stadium. But what was the stadium called when it hosted the first Army-Navy game in 1926?

23. *Joan Specter, city councilwoman:*
Richardson Dilworth resigned as Philadelphia mayor in 1962 to run against William Scranton for governor. But in the midst of the campaign he took a controversial stand that seemed to turn public opinion against him and seal his defeat. What was this controversial position?

24. *David Auspitz, Famous Delicatessen, 4th and Bainbridge St.:*
The Eagles moved into Veterans Stadium in 1971. Can you name all four of their home fields that preceded it?

25. *Steve Fredericks, WCAU-AM sports director:*

The Philadelphia Warriors were the first champions of the professional basketball league now known as the NBA. The scoring leader for that championship 1946-47 team was also the league's scoring leader. Who was he, what college did he attend, and what number did he wear for the Warriors?

26. *Bill Campbell, sports broadcaster:*
    The 1984 Detroit Tigers got off to the greatest start in the history of the majors, with a 35-5 record in their first 40 games. Interestingly, the 1911 Tigers had a similar record-breaking performance to *end* the season, going 31-9 in their last 40 games. Where did the Philadelphia A's finish that season?

27. *Tommy McDonald, president of McDonald Enterprises and former Eagles receiver:*
    I first visited Philadelphia in January 1957 to receive the Maxwell Award and begin discussions on a pro contract with the Eagles. Most of the newspaper and broadcast coverage of my arrival, however, focused on neither of those events. Why did I get so much notoriety on my first visit to Philadelphia?

28. *Dave Zinkoff, veteran sports announcer and voice of the 76ers:*
    Most basketball fans remember Wilt Chamberlain's days with the Warriors, 76ers, and Los Angeles Lakers. But do you remember the fourth pro basketball team that Chamberlain once played for?

7.
Answers

1. Sports

1. Former New York Giants shortstop and Major League manager Alvin Dark.

2. Athletics: Bob Trice, a pitcher who joined the club in 1953. Phillies: John Irwin Kennedy, a third baseman who appeared in five games in 1957. Warriors: Jackie Moore in 1954.

3. The game between the Eagles and Pittsburgh Steelers at Franklin Field on October 11, 1959.

4. Gene Conley, who played for the NBA Boston Celtics and New York Knicks from 1952-64, pitched in the 1957 World Series for the Milwaukee Braves. He played for the Phillies in 1959 and '60. Dick Groat, who had a brief NBA career for the Fort Wayne Pistons in 1952-3, went on to appear in two World Series, for the Pirates in 1960 and the Cardinals in 1964. He played for the Phils in 1966 and '67. Ron Reed played for the Detroit Pistons in 1965-7 before turning to baseball and pitching for the Phils' 1980 and '83 World Series teams.

5. Here are the other seven: Milo Candina, Ken Johnson, Bubba Church, Russ Meyer, Ken Heintzelman, Sylvester Donnelly, and Bob Miller.

6. Manager Dallas Green

7. In 1956 the Warriors beat the Fort Wayne Pistons. The starting five were Paul Arizin, Neil Johnston, Joe Graboski, Jack George, and Tom Gola.

8. Bobby Clarke won the Hart Trophy for most valuable player in 1973, '75, and '76, and the Frank Selke Trophy for best defensive forward in 1983. Bernie Parent won the Conn Smythe Trophy (MVP in the playoffs) in 1974 and '75, and the Vezina Trophy (leading goalie) in 1974 and '75. Reggie Leach won the Conn Smythe Trophy in 1976.

9. He was the first Major League player drafted to fight in Korea.

10. It was formed in 1956. St. Joe's won the first title.

11. Matt Goukas Sr. played for the Warriors in 1946-7, and Matt Goukas Jr. played for the 76ers 20 years later.

12. Hans Lobert managed in 1938 and returned in 1942. Eddie Sawyer was rehired in 1958 after being fired in 1952. And general manager Paul Owens took control of field management in both 1972 and 1983.

13. Richie Ashburn won in 1955 and '58. Ferris Fain led the American League in 1951 and '52.

14. The Quakers were Philadelphia's first entry in the NHL. During the 1930-31 season the team went 4-36-4, which remains the worst record for any major league hockey team in history.

15. John B. Kelly Sr., Grace and Jack's father, was named for rowing.

16. Gil Turner, of Strawberry Mansion, was TKO'd by Kid Gavilan in a welterweight title fight at Philadelphia's Municipal Stadium.

17. Johnny Saxton.

18. a-8; b-5; c-6; d-7; e-2; f-3; g-9; h-4; i-l.

19. Temple won the 1938 N.I.T. tournament.

20. The season ended with an elimination tournament to decide who would represent the United States at the 1952 Summer Olympics. N.C.A.A. champ Kansas, with Clyde Lovellette, beat LaSalle and went on to play Peoria, the A.A.U. champs.

21. Tailback and team captain Francis "Reds" Bagnell. During his brilliant season, Bagnell established two national records. He made 88 straight passes without an interception and, in a game against Dartmouth, accounted for 490 total yards — 272 on rushes and the rest through the air.

22. First baseman Eddie Waitkus, who hit .284 after being shot and critically wounded by a deranged young woman.

23. c.

24. Don Money. Ted Sizemore.

25. Del Ennis, who also led the team with 31 home runs and 126 RBIs, hit .311.

26. Harry Silcox.

27. The Phils sent Smoky Burgess, Steve Ridzik, and Stan Palys to Cincinnati in return for Seminick, Jim Greengrass, and Glen Gorbous.

28. Eddie Joost in Philadelphia, and Lou Boudreau in Kansas City.

29. The Galapagos Islands. Phoebe.

30. At the height of World War II, with a lack of manpower on the home front, the franchise was merged with the Pittsburgh Steelers and called, for one season only, the Steagles.

31. His first names, Francis Marion, are the same as those of the Revolutionary War hero known as the "Swamp Fox" for his fighting exploits in the swamps of South Carolina, Campbell's home state. He got the nickname while playing for the University of Georgia.

32. a.

33. Robinson won the World Middleweight Championship, but he was only recognized by the Pennsylvania State Boxing Authority. In a dispute with the New York Commission, Pennsylvania would not recognize Jake LaMotta as the champion and sanctioned the Robinson-Villemain fight to fill the vacant title.

34. Wally Jones, Bill Melchionni, Jim Washington, and Hubie White (Villanova); Cliff Anderson, Steve Courtin, and Matt Goukas (St. Joe's); Joe Bryant, Larry Cannon, and Ken Durrett (La Salle); Dave Wohl (Penn); Jerry Baskerville (Temple).

35. Walter "Buddy" Davis. In June 1952 he set a world's high jump record with a 6' 11½" leap, and went on to win a gold medal in the 1952 Olympics. He later played back-up center for the Warriors behind NBA scoring leader Neil Johnston.

36. Their last NFL championship game was in 1960 against Green Bay. But the team's last

postseason game came a year later, when they finished second in the East and appeared in the now-defunct Playoff Bowl. They lost to Detroit 39-10.

37. a) Frank Kilroy; b) Ben Hawkins; c) Dennis Harrison; d) Coach Earle Neale; e) Norm Van Brocklin; f) Cliff Patton; g) Norm Willey; h) Chuck Bednarik; i) Harold Giancanilli; j) Coach Lawrence Shaw.

38. He hit four home runs in a row, the first National Leaguer to do so since Bobby Lowe of Boston 82 years earlier. He was the first Major Leaguer to hit four homers in a game since Willie Mays in 1961.

39. Ambrose F. (Bud) Dudley.

40. Adrian Burk and Bobby Thomason.

41. Former Radnor High School star Ted Dean both times. After Green Bay had taken a 13-10 lead in the third quarter, Dean returned the ensuing kickoff 58 yards to the Green Bay 39. He later plunged over from the five-yard line for the winning touchdown.

42. Frank Reagan.

43. He broke his own record of 78, set earlier that year. The previous record holder had been Elgin Baylor, who scored 71 points on November 15, 1960. The game was played in Hershey, Pa.

44. Liberty Bell Park in northeast Philadelphia opened as the first pari-mutual racetrack in the state's history.

45. Dave Philley, who accomplished the same feat in 1958.

46. Rio Grande College, led by Clarence "Bevo" Francis. In the team's first game against a major college opponent, Rio Grande barely lost by a score of 93 to 92.

47. a-4; b-8; c-6; d-1; e-7; f-3; g-5; h-2.

48. On June 23 against Cincinnati, Wise became the only Major League pitcher to hit two home runs in a game while pitching a no-hitter. He later that season tied an N.L. record when he had a second two-homer game.

49. Numbers 15 (Steve Van Buren), 40 (Tom Brookshier), 44 (Pete Retzlaff), 60 (Chuck Bednarik), and 70 (Al Wistert).

50. Earle ("Greasy") Neale, coach of the Eagles' 1948 and '49 NFL championship teams, was also coach for Washington and Jefferson in the 1922 Rose Bowl. He also played outfield for Cincinnati in the 1919 "Black Sox" World Series.

51. Whitey Lockman, Jackie Robinson, and Stan Musial.

52. All four men suited up for both teams in that game. When the game started on November 8, 1978, Catchings and Simpson were members of the Sixers, and Money and Skinner were with New Jersey. With five minutes and 50 seconds left in the third quarter, Bernard King and Coach Kevin Loughery of the Nets each received their third technical foul. Though the Sixers went on to apparently win the game, 137-133, the Nets later protested: NBA rules state that a player must leave the game after

receiving a second technical foul. The protest was upheld, and the game was replayed four months later from the time of the incident. In between, the teams had made a trade and the four had switched uniforms.

53. The Philadelphia Uhrik Truckers, who played at the old Lighthouse Field at Front St. and Erie Ave.

54. Here are the 50 athletes whose last names can be found. *From the Phillies:* Larry Bowa, Willie Montanez, Dick Allen, Jack Sanford, Pete Rose, Gene Mauch, Jim Bunning, Ray Culp, Tony Gonzalez, Clay Dalrymple, Bake McBride, Peanuts Lowrey, Ron Reed, Steve Carlton. *A's:* Wally Moses, Elmer Valo. *Eagles:* Pete Pihos, Bobby Walston, Toy Ledbetter, Jim Ringo, Alex Wojciechowicz, Sonny Jurgensen, Bill Bradley, Sam Baker, Tom Dempsey, Tim Rossovich, Leroy Keyes, Jim Kuharich, Harold Carmichael. *Warriors:* Paul Arizin, Neil Johnston, Guy Rodgers, George Senesky, Wilt Chamberlain. *76ers:* Chet Walker, Hal Greer, Woody Sauldsberry, Billy Cunningham, Doug Collins, Julius Erving. *Flyers:* Don Blackburn, Terry Crisp, Gary Dornhoefer, Orest Kindrachuk, Andre Lacroix, Dave Schultz. *Stars:* Kelvin Bryant. *Boxing:* Jersey Joe Walcott, Joey Girardella, Joe Frazier.

(See following page.)

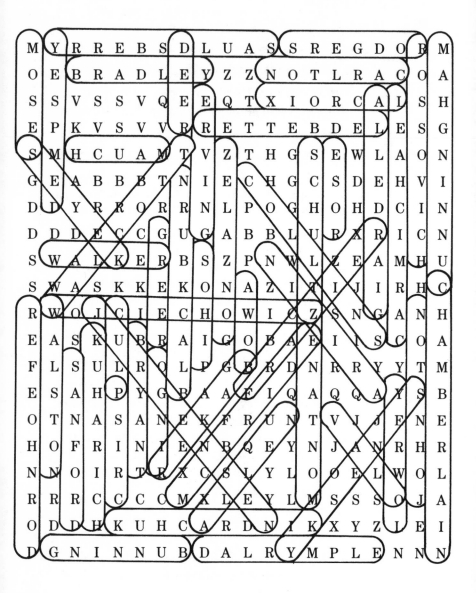

M Y R R E B S D L U A S S R E G D O R M
O E B R A D L E Y Z Z N O T L R A C O A
S S V S S V Q E E Q T X I O R C A I S H
E P K V S V V R R E T T E B D E L E S G
S M H C U A M T V Z T H G S E W L A O N
G E A B B B T N I E C H G C S D E H V I
D D Y R R O R R N L P O G H O H D C I N
D D D E C C G U G A B B L U R R I C N N
S W A L K E R B S Z P N W L Z E A M H U
S W A S K K E K O N A Z I I I J I R H C
R W O J C I E C H O W I C Z S N G A N H
E A S K U B R A I G O B A E I I S C O A
F L S U L R O L P G E R D N R R Y Y T M
E S A H P Y G B A A F I Q A Q Q A Y S B
O T N A S A N E K F R U N T V I J E N E
H O F R I N I E N B Q E Y N J A N R H R
N N O I R T R X C S L Y L O O E L W O L
R R R C C C M X L E Y L M S S O J A
O D D H K U H C A R D N I K X Y Z L E I
D G N I N N U B D A L R Y M P L E N N

2. Media

1. Bob Horn and Lee Stewart.

2. *Action in the Afternoon.* Sometimes when the Indians were attacking, you could see the "E" bus go by on City Line.

3. Ernie Kovacs and Edie Adams.

4. Stan Lee Broza was the emcee. Some of the people who started on his show were Ezra Stone (radio's original Henry Aldrich), Ann Sheridan, Red Benson, Buddy DeFranco, Elliot Lawrence, Eddie Fisher, and Kitty Kallen.

5. Mort Farr did the commercials on *The Frank Brookhouser Show.*

6. George Walsh was the sportscaster, and *George Walsh Looks 'em Over* was his show. Tom Moorehead was the radio man.

7. Jan Peerce's *Bluebird of Happiness.* The announcer was Joe McCauley. Requests were made by telegram.

8. Here are six: *Saturday Evening Post, Ladies Home Journal, American Home, Holiday, Jack & Jill,* and *Country Gentleman.*

9. Here are 12: *American Ukrainian Catholic Daily, German-American Newspaper, Gwiazda* (Polish), *Il Popolo Italiano, Sons of Italy Times, Irish Edition, Jewish Daily Forward, Jewish Exponent, Jewish Times of the Greater Northeast, Korea Guardian, Jersey Star* (black), *Philadelphia Tribune* (black), *Mir* (Russian), and *The Truth* (Russian).

10. The white youths were protesting a CBS News documentary on the Black Panthers.

11. By Saam and Bill Campbell worked the Quakers' games for WCAU, and Tom Moorehead did them on WFIL. Jim Leaming handled the Wildcats' games.

12. Donald L. Bartlett and James B. Steele of the *Inquirer* won for national reporting, for their series describing inequities in the federal tax system.

13. WIBG — "I believe in God." WJMJ — "Jesus, Mary, and Joseph."

14. Joe would play pop tunes on his organ, sometimes for as much as 15 minutes. Ed referred to Joe as "the little fat boy from Roxborough." Joe called Ed "Dimples."

15. WMMR-FM.

16. a-5; b-7; c-10; d-1; e-9; f-2; g-4; h-6; i-15; j-3; k-14; l-9; m-11; n-13; o-12.

17. Carl McIntyre.

18. The transaction represented the joining of America's first television station (established in 1932 as experimental station W3XE) with the nation's first radio broadcasters.

19. KYW and WRCV.

20. The story was based on an escaped inmate's revelations of brutality at Fairview State Hospital, the subject of a Pulitzer Prize-winning series of articles in the *Philadelphia Inquirer*.

21. A telecast of Channel 3's show *Telekids* marked the first time a live theater audience was shown on television.

22. Founded in 1949, *TV Digest* later became the Philadelphia edition of *TV Guide*.

23. His full name is Ora Traynor Halftown. He opened by saying, *"Hi-chee e sta sussessaway"* ("Hello, friends, let's get started"). He closed with a simple *"Oh-neh"* ("farewell").

24. Organist Larry Ferrari, then 20 years old, was the host, and his show was *Fort Dix Presents*.

25. Bertie the Bunyip and his little friend Nixie the Pixie.

26. The show was *Lunch With Uncle Pete*, and the man was Pete Boyle. Snooper was the friendly rodent.

27. a-2; b-1; c-3.

28. Jack Whitaker.

29. a) Alan Scott; b) Ed Harvey and Nancy Dolphin; c) Tom Moorehead; d) Allen Stone; e) Tom Moorehead; f) Jack Valentine; g) Pat Landon.

30. a-3; b-4; c-8; d-1; e-6; f-2; g-5; h-7.

31. *Kitchen Kapers*.

32. Jack Sterling was the ringmaster of the show, which originated from the Camden Convention Hall. Bill Hart was possibly the tallest clown (without stilts) in circus history.

33. Jack Fried, longtime boxing editor of the *Philadelphia Bulletin*, used the pen name Nat Ring.

34. She was married to Jesse Rogers, who had appeared on network TV as Ranger Joe.

35. Esslinger.

36. Magnolia Blossom and Albert.

37. KYW.

38. Marv Pollow and Doan-Calhoun.

39. Susan Peters, confined to a wheelchair, was the leading lady on *Miss Susan*.

40. The "P" stands for Philadelphia; the "VI" is the Roman numeral six, for the station's channel number.

41. As a reporter for the *Bulletin*, he shared the 1964 Pulitzer Prize for local reporting with James V. Magle and Frederick A. Meyer.

42. "Miss Terry" was Theresa Ann Delany, the seven-month-old daughter of Mr. and Mrs. Hugh Delany of West Philadelphia. She became a regular on Channel 3's *Skinner Spotlight* on November 16, 1953, and audiences watched her cry, coo, and get changed each day until she was age four. At that time her mother decided it was time for Theresa to give up show business and return to a normal life.

43. The show was *Get Happy*, featuring Jack Valentine, the Tommy Fergusen Trio, and singer Sandy Stewart.

44. Jean Shepherd.

45. Assigned to report the daily missing-persons announcements, Morgan one day reported that one of the station's owners was missing with

his pockets full of money. It was a joke, but the station didn't laugh.

46. Bob Menefee and Jack Pyle.

47. a) Carol Reed; b) Lynn Barrett; c) Mary Wilson.

48. Doug Arthur used his own name at WIBG and called himself Art Douglas at WIP.

49. Gene Kelly, By Saam, and Claude Haring.

3. Entertainment, Recreation, and Dining

1. On Walnut St. between 13th and Juniper. Philadelphia's first Holiday Inn is there now.

2. Lew Tendler, who never won a title but fought and beat some of the best. The *Barry Gray Show* and the *Steve Allison Show.*

3. The Pearl, at 21st and Ridge; the Nixon Grand Opera House, on Broad and Montgomery; the Lincoln, on Broad and Lombard; and the Uptown, on Broad and Dauphin, the only one that still stands.

4. New Circus. Equestrian and other circus acts.

5. Milan's La Scala opera house. The Grand Old Lady of Broad Street.

6. On Woodside Ave., just east of Monument Rd. The Wildcat and the Tornado.

7. Kelly's, on 12th St. across from the Reading Terminal.

8. The Click.

9. Sciolla's.

10. Lillian Reis.

11. 808 Chestnut St. It closed in December 1968.

12. It was the Benjamin Franklin Hotel's featured attraction, an ice show filled with lavish production numbers and comedy routines.

13. Sam Framo, whose restaurant at 23rd and Allegheny hosted many parties before and after games at Shibe Park. In ads, Sam was always shown in chef hat, bow tie, and sport jacket, giving a jaunty two-fingered salute.

14. The "Fabulous" Miss Julie Gibson. The "Dance of the Bashful Bride."

15. "Pop" Lubin made Philadelphia the site of the first full-time motion picture studio in the country. As a pioneer film producer, Lubin gave such stars as Marie Dressler and Evelyn Nesbit their start in movies. Among his other accomplishments, Lubin produced the first fight films and created some of the earliest movie stunts.

16. a-1; b-4; c-5; d-3; e-2.

17. *The Big Broadcast of 1937.*

18. On conveyer belts.

19. A computer-created boxing match between Rocky Marciano and Muhammad Ali on January 20, 1970.

20. a-2; b-3; c-4; d-1.

21. The Wilson Line.

22. They were attractions at Willow Grove Amusement Park.

23. a-3; b-9; c-5; d-8; e-7; f-2; g-1; h-4; i-6; j-14; k-12; l-10; m-11; n-13.

24. The Erie Social Club.

25. They were all strippers who appeared regularly at the Troc Theater.

26. Capt. Starn's, Neptune Inn, Abe's, Hackney's, and Doc's.

27. Fralinger's Original and James' Original.

28. Nelson Eddy and Jeanette MacDonald.

29. Mickey Mouse, in Disney's *Fantasia*.

30. Bob Russell, who had emceed the pageant for many years in the 1940s, came back to host the pageant in 1954, the year before Parks made his debut. Bob Evans, former lead vocalist for Fred Waring and his Pennsylvanians, preceded Russell.

31. Massa, who was born in December 1929.

32. The Opera Company of Philadelphia and tenor Luciano Pavarotti.

33. Levis, on 6th St. between Lombard and South.

34. a) Benjamin Franklin; b) Warwick; c) Bellevue Stratford; d) Penn Sherwood (Philadelphian); e) Hamilton Court; f) Essex Hotel.

35. Designated as a landmark, the theater now shows Chinese movies and other cultural

presentations. The Carmen and the Fays.

36. The John B. Kelly Playhouse in the Park, which opened on July 30, 1952.

37. The Philadelphia Auditorium and Ice Palace.

38. *Stalag 17.*

39. a) Chalfonte-Haddon Hall; b) Hamid; c) The Diving Horse and the General Motors exhibit.

40. a-3; b-1; c-6; d-5; e-4; f-2.

41. *The Blob*, starring Steve McQueen.

42. *A Raisin in the Sun*, by Lorraine Hansberry. The stars included Sidney Poitier, Diana Sands, Ruby Dee, and Claudia McNeil.

43. Stanley Mastbaum, who teamed with his brother Jules to assemble one of Philadelphia's largest and most successful movie theater chains.

44. The Tastykake.

45. It is the nation's oldest amateur Gilbert and Sullivan troupe.

46. *The Lights of New York*, with Helen Costello, which opened at the Stanley Theater on August 20, 1928. *The Jazz Singer* played earlier (at the Fox-Locust in November 1927), but it employed sound only partially.

47. The Boardwalk's famous hand-pushed wicker rolling chairs.

48. Benjamin Harrison, who used Cape May Point as his summer White House from 1893-97.

49. Bill Bailey was considered by many to be one of the greatest tap dancers of all time.

4. Places and Geography

1. Municipal Stadium and Pennsylvania Boulevard.

2. The Chinese Wall was a two-story open-air brick structure that occupied a block-wide area between JFK Blvd. and Market St. and ran from the Schuylkill River to 15th St. It served as a viaduct for passenger trains to travel from the area where 30th Street Station now stands to the center of the city.

3. The John Bartram Hotel and (earlier) the Hotel Walton. The dining room was Jack Lynch's Walton Roof.

4. It was so named because it lies along the Pennsylvania Railroad's main rail line to Chicago and points west.

5. To the middle of the Grand Court of the main store of John Wanamaker's, next to the large sculpture of an eagle. The eagle, incidentally, was bought by the store in 1904 from the city of St. Louis, where it had been part of the world's fair that year.

6. The eternal flame is a tribute to the unknown soldier of the Revolutionary War. Many unmarked Revolutionary War graves also are within the park.

7. It was called Wilson Airport, in honor of former Philadelphia Mayor S. David Wilson, who died in office in 1939.

8. a) Essex; b) Ritz-Carlton; c) Adelphia;
    d) Penn Sherwood (Philadelphian);
    e) Senator; f) Normandie; g) Sylvania.

9. They are the original Market St. subway and
    elevated train stops: 2nd St., 5th St., 8th St.,
    etc., up to the 69th St. Terminal.

10. William Shakespeare. "All the world's a stage
    and all the men and women merely players."

11. Boies Penrose, a native Philadelphian who
    served as U.S. senator from 1897 to 1921.

12. John E. Reyburn, mayor of Philadelphia from
    1907 to 1911.

13. It is the largest fresh-water port in the world

14. Pennsylvania is spelled "Pensylvania."

15. a-4; b-8; c-6; d-3; e-7; f-1; g-2; h-5; i-10; j-9.

16. Theater magnate Jules E. Mastbaum, who
    planned it and donated it but never lived to see
    it opened to the public in 1929.

17. The others are county, not city, parks, and,
    unlike Fairmount, are not continuously land-
    scaped spaces.

18. The Thomas Mill Road Bridge over the
    Wissahickon in Fairmount Park, about a half-
    mile below Bell's Mill Road.

19. Old Moyamensing Prison.

20. Broad Street Station.

21. Leary's Book Store.

22. The Afro-American Historical and Cultural
    Museum; the American-Swedish Historical
    Museum; the Museum of American Jewish

History; and the Museum for the Balch Institute (part of the Balch Institute for Ethnic Studies).

23. Centre (Penn) Square, Southeast (Washington) Square, Northeast (Logan) Square, Southwest (Rittenhouse) Square, and Northwest (Franklin) Square.

24. Philadelphia, Chester, Montgomery, Bucks, and Delaware in Pennsylvania. Camden, Burlington, and Gloucester in New Jersey.

25. The famous RCA Victor trademark of a dog listening to his master's voice on a phonograph. The landmark had stood for 53 years.

26. The Calders. With Alexander Calder's mobile *The Ghost* overhead in the East Foyer of the museum, one can look out a window and see the Swann Memorial Fountain in Logan Square, the work of his father, Alexander Stirling Calder, as well as the statue of William Penn atop City Hall, the work of his grandfather, Alexander Milne Calder.

27. Philadelphian Charles Allen Smith, the second American killed at Vera Cruz in 1914.

28. Grace's dress is in the Philadelphia Museum of Art, on a mannequin donated by Gimbel's. The racing shell is at the Franklin Institute.

29. It uses the figure IIII instead of IV.

30. The Frankford Ave., or Pennypack, Bridge in Holmesburg. Built in 1697 across the Pennypack Creek, it was part of King's Highway between Philadelphia and New York.

31. Grant's cabin, which he used as his headquarters during the Siege of Richmond in 1864.

32. Lit Brothers, Snellenberg's, Blauner's, and Frank & Seder.

33. The Schuylkill Navy.

34. The U.S. Marine Corps was organized there by Captain Samuel Nicholas on November 10, 1775.

35. Mother Bethel African Methodist Episcopal Church at 419 South 6th St. The congregation has occupied four buildings on the same site since 1787.

36. d. The Pla-Mor was in Kansas City, Mo.

37. The Ambassador, Brighton, Chalfonte-Hadden Hall, Claridge, Dennis, Malborough-Blenheim, Senator, President, Shelburne, and Traymore.

38. Saint John Neumann is enshrined in a glass tomb at St. Peter's, located at 5th and Girard. The only other native American saint, Mother Seton, is buried out of view in Baltimore.

39. b. The city of Gloucester, strange as it seems, is in Camden County.

40. Longport, N.J.

41. The No. 23 trolley, which runs 14 miles from Chestnut Hill to 10th and Bigler in South Philly. If the wind is with you, the trip takes about 90 minutes.

42. Fishtown, the lower part of Kensington centered on East Girard Ave.

43. It is believed that the name originated in 1867

when the Pennsylvania Railroad built its station over a brook in that area.

44. Moyamensing Ave.

45. It is the oldest museum and school of art in the country.

46. Paris's Champs Elysees.

47. Red Arrow's Ardmore trolley, which ran from 69th St. to their area.

5. People, Events, and Potpourri

1. He grew up at 11th and Green and went to Temple, playing on the Temple football teams of the late 1950s.

2. In 1932 Capone was seized carrying a concealed weapon. He was held in Eastern State Penitentiary.

3. Philadelphians shouldn't be surprised that the word comes from the Greek and means "brotherly love." The motto is "Philadelphia Maneto," which means "Let brotherly love continue."

4. They are the three Philadelphia natives to be crowned Miss America — Malcomson in 1924, Coyle in 1936, and Burke in 1940.

5. The Pitcairn Aviation Co. was a locally based aviation pioneer (it was the inventor of the autogiro) that provided mail service between New York and Atlanta from 1928 to 1930. The

company was later sold to a New York group and changed its name to Eastern Air Transport. It eventually became Eastern Air Lines.

6. The winds tore holes in the roof of the newly built Spectrum—the first time with 11,000 people inside, the second time when it was empty—sparking a dispute over the quality of the building's construction.

7. The last one held in Philadelphia was the Progressive Party's 1948 convention, on July 23-24, which nominated Henry Wallace. The last President to be nominated in Philadelphia was Harry Truman, whom the Democrats nominated just a week earlier, on July 12-15. In fact, the Republicans came to Philadelphia that year, too, June 21-24, to nominate Thomas E. Dewey.

8. The Walnut Street Theater.

9. His friendship with Billie Jean King, who was then coach of the Philadelphia Freedoms tennis team.

10. Mario Lanza. It is located at 221 Queen St. in South Philly.

11. George M. Leader, who was stepping down as governor.

12. She helped lay the keel of the Savannah, the world's first commercial nuclear vessel.

13. George M. Leader of Pennsylvania and Robert B. Meyner of New Jersey.

14. "Rowbottoms." At a secretly predetermined moment, someone would yell the word "Rowbottom" from a dorm window, signaling

a campuswide outburst of merrymaking and prankish acts.

15. She was in Monaco to attend the wedding of Grace Kelly and Prince Rainier III.

16. a) Rev. Daniel Poling; b) Thatcher Longstreth; c) Harold Stassen; d) James McDermott; e) Arlen Spector; f) Thatcher Longstreth; g) Thomas Fogliatti; h) David Marston; i) John Egan.

17. It was the name for the first civil defense evacuation drill in the country, which took place in Philadelphia on November 23, 1954. Some 25,000 city employees and office workers participated by walking from City Hall to 21st and the Parkway.

18. On March 28 the Tidewater Grain Co., at 30th and Market was leveled by an explosion that killed three people, injured 84, and damaged many nearby buildings. On April 19, Sun Oil's new ammonia plant at Marcus Hook exploded. No one was killed, but many were injured.

19. U.S. Congressman William S. Green, father of the former mayor.

20. Archbishop (later Cardinal) John F. O'Hara took charge of the Philadelphia Archdiocese.

21. a) Chubby Checker; b) W.C. Fields; c) Elaine May; d) Mario Lanza; e) Nancy Walker.

22. Temple University, with approximately 9,500 employees at the main campus and Health Sciences Center.

23. Werner Erhard, the founder of est.

24. Harold E. Stassen, former top man at the University of Pennsylvania.

25. Casey.

26. The seven-foot "Bundy Giant," Mike Stiegler, who wore a sandwich board advertising Bundy's typewriter store on that corner.

27. It was the only bullfight ever staged in Philadelphia. The "bloodless" exhibition was put on to show that the sport could be nonviolent, in hopes that it would be legally sanctioned. But Judge Griffiths ruled that Pennsylvania law prohibits such events and enjoined any future exhibitions.

28. Mayor Richardson Dilworth resigned to run for governor. As president of the city council, Tate automatically assumed the office.

29. The bill, signed in July 1967, allowed merchants (in this case Jewish) to open their shops on Sunday if they closed them on Saturday, thus circumventing the "blue laws."

30. He was the last horse in the U.S. Navy. He died at the age of 34 at the old Naval Home in Philadelphia on July 11, 1968.

31. Glassboro State Teachers College was selected for the meeting between Lyndon Johnson and Soviet Premier Alexei Kosygin because it was exactly halfway between New York and Washington, where the two men were coming from.

32. Tony Randall.

33. The court upheld lower court rulings that Girard College had to admit black students,

despite the specifications of Stephen Girard's will, which stated that the school was for "poor, white, male orphans."

34. The 20-car train bearing the body of Sen. Robert F. Kennedy, which was making its way from New York to Washington for the funeral.

35. They were murdered. Their bodies were found 100 yards off the Garden State Parkway in Somer's Point, but the case has never been solved.

36. Fields was one of several celebrities asked by *Vanity Fair* magazine to write a comic epitaph for themselves. Fields submitted: "Here lies W.C. Fields. I would rather be living in Philadelphia."

37. It is Philadelphia's black police organization. It gave Evers $6,000 and a police car for his city.

38. Sir Walter Scott used Rebecca Gratz, a member of Philadelphia's Gratz family, as his model for Rebecca in Ivanhoe. She is buried in Mikveh Israel Cemetery.

39. The first parade was in 1876, but the first one that resembled the present-day parade (with Broad St. as the setting) was in 1901.

40. Captain Ferguson was one of the most honored and beloved policemen in Philadelphia history. He holds the record of the most arrests by one officer in his career.

41. Andrew Wyeth, who dined with the Nixons on February 19, 1970.

42. George M. Dallas, who served under James K. Polk from 1845-49.

43. Manny Rosenfeld and the brothers Moe and Jack Strauss. Jack later opened the Strauss Stores in New York City.

44. b.

45. P.R.T. (Philadelphia Rapid Transit).

46. Gen. Henry "Hap" Arnold, the namesake for Lower Merion's "Hap" Arnold Field.

47. ENIAC, which stood for Electronic Numerical Integrator and Computer.

48. Municipal Judge Edwin Helfant was shot to death as he sat in the restaurant of the Flamingo Motel. A man apparently came through the door carrying a snow shovel, suddenly raised a shotgun, and killed the judge. The crime was never solved.

49. Provident National Bank — b, e, g, h. Philadelphia National Bank — f, i. Fidelity Bank — c, d. Girard Bank — a.

50. a) Belmont; b) Chestnut; c) Kingsley; d) Market; e) Pennypacker; f) Germantown; g) Evergreen; h) Victor; i) Trinity; j) Orchard; k) Jefferson; l) Howard.

6. Guest Shots

1. At the top of the steps on the north side facing Broad St.

2. Memorial Hall at 42nd and Parkside, which now houses the Fairmount Park Commission and Park Unit Police.

3. Buster Mathis was the finalist whom I replaced. Although I won the gold medal, I broke my wrist during the competition in Japan.

4. The Bijou burlesque theater.

5. Stein was the first publisher in Philadelphia to invite the union to organize employees at his newspaper.

6. Michael Marcuse (1975-82), Matthew Costango (1971-75), Mark Shedd (1967-71), C. Taylor Whitter (1964-67), Allen H. Wetter (1955-64).

7. Frank LeMaster intercepted a pass on the New York Giants' 10-yard line and went over for the touchdown, as the Eagles won 20-3.

8. Tommy Thompson (Eagles, 1944-50), Gypsy Joe Harris (boxer, 1975-80), Barry Ashby (Flyers, 1970-74).

9. "The Cisco Kid." When I arrived at a holdup scene, I saw an armed man running from the area. As I jumped from the police car and began to chase him, a teenager on the corner yelled, "The Cisco Kid will get him!"

10. Frank Sinatra, the "Chairman of the Board" disguised in a beard.

11. Opera. She appeared with the Philadelphia Civic Opera Company as Marguerite in Gounod's *Faust*.

12. Clayton played basketball with the Harlem Globetrotters in 1940-41 and 1945-46.

13. Cecil B. DeMille's *The Greatest Show on Earth*.

14. Virginia Knauer (1960), Bea Chernock (1972), and Esther Allen (1972).

15. Carl Robie (swimming, 1968), Joe Frazier (boxing, 1964), Don Bragg (pole vault, 1960), Charlie Jenkins (400 meter run, 1956), Joe Verdeur (swimming, 1948), Paul Costello (rowing, 1920, '24, '28), Jack Kelly Sr. (rowing, 1920, '24), Vespers Boat Club (rowing, 1900, '04, '64).

16. *Big Top, Candy Carnival, Action in the Afternoon, In the Park, Summer School, What in the World?, Ranger Joe,* and *Willie the Worm* were among the most popular.

17. Arlen Specter, who was a registered Democrat at the time of the election, but officially changed parties on December 29, 1965.

18. Jack Kemp, now U.S. congressman from New York.

19. Sunday sales of alcoholic beverages became legal on January 7, 1960. But each municipality that qualified had to approve the sales in a special referendum in which at least 25 percent of the registered voters approved. The process took a few months, and the first legal Sunday drink in Philadelphia was not taken until June 15, 1960.

20. Until the late 1930s, the Eagles' colors matched those of the city of Philadelphia, blue and gold. The National Recovery Act (NRA), which used the eagle as its symbol, inspired Philadelphia to adopt the same symbol for its team.

21. John Madden, who played college ball at Cal

Poly and was selected by the Eagles on the 21st round of the 1958 draft. A knee injury suffered in training camp ended his career with the team.

22. Sesqui-Centennial Stadium, which was renamed Municipal Stadium in 1928.

23. Dilworth proposed that the United States recognize Red China.

24. Franklin Field (1958-71), Shibe Park/Connie Mack Stadium (1940-58), Municipal Stadium (1936-40), and Baker Bowl (1933-36).

25. Joe Fulks, who averaged just over 23 points per game. Fulks played for Murray State Teachers College in Kentucky, and wore No. 10 for Eddie Gottlieb's Warriors.

26. Despite the Tigers' great finish, they still wound up 13½ games behind the pennant-winning A's.

27. When I went to the airline office to confirm my return reservations, I was mistaken by a clerk for a holdup man known as the ''kissing bandit.'' Detectives handcuffed me and were prepared to make an arrest, but a phone call to Vince McNally of the Eagles convinced them I wasn't their man. I later received a letter of apology from Mayor Dilworth.

28. The Harlem Globetrotters. Wilt did not complete his senior year of college, but because of NBA rules could not join the Warriors until his class graduated. He played with the Globetrotters in the interim.

Bernard Stiefel was born on June 22, 1937, in Philadelphia's St. Luke's Hospital. While growing up, he lived on Rittenhouse Square and at 47th and Pine in West Philadelphia, and later in Merion and Wynnewood. A 1955 graduate of Lower Merion High School, he received a B.A. degree from Lafayette College in Easton, and attended the University of Pennsylvania's Wharton Graduate School of Business. He earned an MBA from New York University's Graduate School of Business Administration.

After an absence of more than 14 years, Stiefel returned to Philadelphia in 1975, where he worked for five years as a marketing executive in the financial services industry. He lived at Queen Village, and had a "place at the shore" in Longport.

Bernie—or "Sonny," as he is known to many of his Philadelphia friends and associates—is the only son of Sam and Bert Stiefel. His father was one of the city's leading owners of vaudeville houses and movie theaters. His mother, the former Alberta Miller, was a former fashion model who became a leading Hollywood hostess during the family's years in California.

Stiefel is now a principal partner in Stiefel, Kerner and Co., a New York-based communications, promotional, and public relations company that specializes in marketing-oriented projects and events for corporate and nonprofit clients.